Animals by the Seashore

by Joanne Ruelos Diaz   illustrated by Simon Mendez

PICTURE WINDOW BOOKS
a capstone imprint

It's a beautiful day at the beach!
Seabirds soar above crystal blue water
while waves tumble onto soft white sand.

Each day and night, the surface of the ocean rises
and falls. When the tide comes in, the water is high
and covers the sand. When the tide goes out, more
of the shore can be seen.

Over and under the waves, incredible wildlife can
be found. From crawling crabs to diving dolphins,
there are so many surprises at the seashore.

Contents

Sunrise
04-05

On the Sand
18-19

The Tide Pool
06-07

Sunset on the Shore
20-21

Over the Waves
08-09

Dusk in the Forest
22-23

Sunny Sand Dunes
10-11

Moonrise over the Water
24-25

Soaring in the Sun
12-13

Spotlight on Sanibel Island
26-27

Underwater
14-15

Creature Features
28-29

Lazy Afternoon
16-17

Glossary and Index
30-31

Waves tickle the shore
as the first beams of
sunlight touch the
sky. Shelled creatures
sprinkle the sand,
ready to start the day.

4

A sand dollar creeps around the shore.

Roseate spoonbills wade in the shallow water.

The lightning whelk looks for breakfast.

A loggerhead sea turtle lays her eggs.

The sun peeks
over the horizon
and a softly glowing
sky stretches over
the tide pools.

Sea stars cling to the rocks. Their hard, spiny skin protects them.

Sea urchins, the prickly porcupines of the sea, graze on green algae.

A horseshoe crab uses its tail to help it move.

The giant loggerhead sponge feeds on plankton.

Can You See?
Sea cucumbers are related to sea stars and sea urchins. Can you find one?

Waves slap the shore as animals splash in and out of the water. The sun rises higher overhead.

Playful dolphins spring up and leap over the waves.

A hungry pelican swoops down to scoop a fish out of the water.

The scales of the giant tarpon fish sparkle in the sun.

The sneaky frigate bird steals another bird's food.

Over in the sand dunes, land-dwelling critters crawl and snooze in the grasses.

The Sanibel Island rice rat rests during the day.

Other animals stay away from the venomous Eastern coral snake.

If this ground skink spots the snake, it will hide under a blanket of leaves.

A gopher tortoise crawls toward its cozy burrow.

Beautiful birds fly across the sky and dive toward the sunlit water. Splash!

Seagulls chatter while they look for food to catch or steal.

Ospreys plunge feet-first into the waves below to snatch fish.

Gliding close to the water, the tern dips its bill into the ocean to take a sip.

A bald eagle calls out over the shore to find possible mates.

Can You See?
Dragonflies are very good fliers. They can move forward and backward. Can you find the incredible insect?

At its highest point in the sky, the heat from the sun is strong. Underwater, the sea creatures keep cool.

The hammerhead shark's eyes help it see all around.

Cownose rays glide through the water.

This octopus can change color if it wants to hide.

Seahorses like to eat! They graze all day.

Slow-moving manatees munch on sea grass.

The male pipefish incubates the eggs in his pouch after the female lays them.

The sea snail pulls its body slowly along the sea floor.

Small sea animals called barnacles fasten themselves to the rocks.

A **warm** afternoon
breeze blows as
high tide rolls in.
Waves grow higher,
splashing along the
rocky shore.

Can You See?
The Moray eel slinks around coral reefs
and rocky areas in shallow waters. Can
you find the snake-like animal?

As the sun
drops, shadows
grow longer across
the warm sand.

The male ghost crab uses its legs to dig a homey hole.

A long-horned sand flea is hard to spot on the shore.

Female kelp flies flock to rotting seaweed to lay their eggs.

A black-bellied plover whistles to other birds.

It's twilight in the mangrove forest, where creatures settle in for the evening.

The American alligator's tail helps it glide quickly through the water.

With sticky foot-pads, the green anole easily crawls along a tree trunk.

Red mangrove tree crabs rest on a branch.

The mangrove periwinkle snail scrapes up algae with its tiny teeth.

The moon beams
brightly over the
shimmering sea.
Many animals rest.
For others, the night
is just beginning.

The great horned
owl hunts at night.

Comb jellies drift
through the water.
Their special
bodies glow.

At the water's
edge, a night
heron looks for fish.

The clever hermit
crab finds a sturdy
shell to hide in.

Spotlight on Sanibel Island

The animals and plants featured in this book live on and around Sanibel Island, Florida.

EUROPE

AFRICA

SOUTH AMERICA

NORTH AMERICA

SOUTH AMERICA

Sanibel Island is shaped like a shrimp! Its unique location makes it a great place to find seashells.

Barrier islands like Sanibel have many habitats for different types of plants and animals to live.

More than half of Sanibel Island is a nature preserve. Animals and plants are protected here.

Sanibel Island is a long, thin, sandy stretch of land that is located off the coast of Florida. Between the island and the mainland is a calm body of water that is home to some amazing creatures.

FLORIDA

Sanibel Island

The J.N. "Ding" Darling National Wildlife Refuge is home to endangered and threatened animals.

Rotting mangrove leaves provide food for animals such as shrimp, crabs, snails, and worms.

Some of Sanibel Island's famous seashells are home to living creatures like hermit crabs.

Creature Features

Animals at the seashore have extraordinary bodies that help them survive in the wild. Match each picture to the correct animal description and learn a few more facts along the way!

D. gopher tortoise

A. lightning whelk

E. hammerhead shark

C. frigate bird

B. horseshoe crab

F. ghost crab

1. If this animal loses its big claw, it can grow a new one.

2. These flat creatures are usually purple or blue. But their skeletons are white.

3. This critter gets its name from the zigzag pattern on its shell.

4. These animals can have five arms or more.

5. This fork-tailed animal is also called a man-o'-war bird.

6. This cool creature is more closely related to a spider than to a crab.

7. These birds of prey have great eyesight. They can spot fish from far away.

8. The front legs of this animal are shaped like shovels.

9. This sea creature uses its uniquely shaped head for hunting.

10. This animal has a venomous tail.

G. cownose ray

I. sea star

J. bald eagle

H. sand dollar

Answers: 1. F; 2. H; 3. A; 4. I; 5. C; 6. B; 7. J; 8. D; 9. E; 10. G.

Glossary

algae:
type of plant that usually grows in water

burrow:
a hole in the ground made by an animal for shelter

crustacean:
mainly water-dwelling creature with a hard shell

endangered:
a species, or type, of animal that is in danger of dying out

mangrove:
a type of tree with many roots that lives in shallow salty water

plankton:
tiny organisms that float freely in ocean currents and other waters

tide:
the rising and falling of the sea level caused by the moon's effect on Earth

venomous:
poisonous

Index

A
American alligator 23

B
bald eagle 12-13
barnacles 16-17
bioluminescent algae 24-25
black-bellied plover 18-19
burrow 11, 21

C
comb jellies *see jellyfish*
cownose ray 14-15
Cuban tree frog 20-21

D
dolphin 8-9, 20
dragonfly 13

E
Eastern coral snake 10-11
Eastern cottontail rabbit 21

F
Florida bark scorpion 21
frigate bird 8-9

G
ghost crab 19
giant loggerhead sponge 7
gopher tortoise 11
great egret 20-21
great horned owl 24
green anole 22-23
ground skink 10-11

H
hammerhead shark 14-15
hermit crab 24-25
horseshoe crab 6-7

J
jellyfish 15, 24

K
kelp 14-15, 16, 18-19
kelp flies 18-19

L
lightning whelk 5
loggerhead sea turtle 4-5
long-horned sand flea 18-19

M
manatee 16-17
mangrove 22-23
mangrove periwinkle snail
    22-23
mangrove salt marsh snake 22
mangrove snapper 23
moray eel 16-17

N
night heron 24-25

O
octopus 14-15
osprey 13

P
palm tree 20-21
pelican 8-9
pipefish 16-17

R
red mangrove tree crab 22-23
roseate spoonbill 4-5

S
sand dollar 5
Sanibel Island rice rat 10-11

scallop 15
sea cucumber 6-7
sea grass 16-17
sea snail 16-17
sea star 6-7
sea urchin 6-7
seagull 4, 12-13, 16-17, 25
seahorse 15

T
tarpon fish 8-9
tern 13
tide pool 6-7

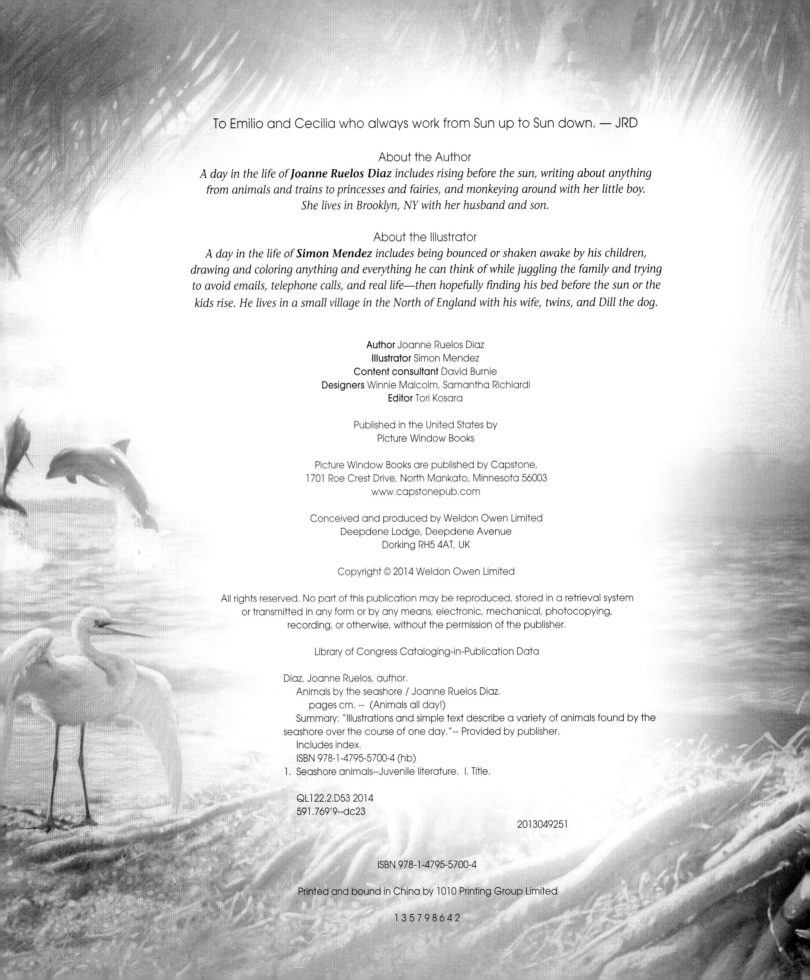

To Emilio and Cecilia who always work from Sun up to Sun down. — JRD

About the Author
*A day in the life of **Joanne Ruelos Diaz** includes rising before the sun, writing about anything from animals and trains to princesses and fairies, and monkeying around with her little boy. She lives in Brooklyn, NY with her husband and son.*

About the Illustrator
*A day in the life of **Simon Mendez** includes being bounced or shaken awake by his children, drawing and coloring anything and everything he can think of while juggling the family and trying to avoid emails, telephone calls, and real life—then hopefully finding his bed before the sun or the kids rise. He lives in a small village in the North of England with his wife, twins, and Dill the dog.*

Author Joanne Ruelos Diaz
Illustrator Simon Mendez
Content consultant David Burnie
Designers Winnie Malcolm, Samantha Richiardi
Editor Tori Kosara

Published in the United States by
Picture Window Books

Picture Window Books are published by Capstone,
1701 Roe Crest Drive, North Mankato, Minnesota 56003
www.capstonepub.com

Conceived and produced by Weldon Owen Limited
Deepdene Lodge, Deepdene Avenue
Dorking RH5 4AT, UK

Library of Congress Cataloging-in-Publication Data

Diaz, Joanne Ruelos, author.
    Animals by the seashore / Joanne Ruelos Diaz.
        pages cm. -- (Animals all day!)
        Summary: "Illustrations and simple text describe a variety of animals found by the
seashore over the course of one day."-- Provided by publisher.
    Includes index.
    ISBN 978-1-4795-5700-4 (hb)
1. Seashore animals--Juvenile literature. I. Title.

QL122.2.D53 2014
591.769'9--dc23
                                                        2013049251

ISBN 978-1-4795-5700-4

Printed and bound in China by 1010 Printing Group Limited

1 3 5 7 9 8 6 4 2